MW01351250

To An

AMAZING TEACHER

I have a ways to go, but it's

a

Made in the USA
Monee, IL
26 July 2023

39943332R00063